ROCKET THINKING

CREATE, BUILD AND SELL

GREAT IDEAS. NOW.

ANDREW WOOLNOUGH

Set in Scala and cover design by Create Alchemy Ltd.

www.create-alchemy.com

Published by Create Alchemy Ltd.

For A&O

FREE SUPPORTING MATERIAL

As a small token of thanks for buying this book, I've created a free and sparky PDF full of practical info to help ignite your own *Rocket Thinking*.

Complementing the tools in this book, these easy to grab and use pages distil key processes and techniques into at-a-glance worksheets and templates.

I've seen first-hand how valuable these can be in amplifying the thinking, managing the process and delivering outstanding results.

Sign up for free to The Rocket List and download your own *Rocket Thinking* materials here:

AndrewWoolnough.com/PBfree

CONTENTS

INTRODUCTION

The objective of this book?
Idea Superpowers for you, now.

Anyone.

This isn't a rule book on 'how to be creative'. Not a set of instructions for the creative team, the designer, the director or the 'crazy thinker' we all know. It's not about the abstract concept of ideas, or the academic evaluation of them.

No. Regardless of your background or job, this is a collection of practical, proven and powerful ways to create, build and sell great ideas, now.

More than two thirds of the world are awake right now. Billions of people going about their business, working, thinking and creating.

Right now, the innovations of the future are being crafted. Someone is developing a simple idea into the next must-have product you'll buy, or that app that will be on everyone's phones next year.

Ideas permeate everything we do. They arrive and depart with lightning speed like solar neutrinos and nothing will get in their way.

Ideas ignite a simple spark, lighting the fuse, launching the rocket. That beautiful firework of thinking that we craft into actions, plans, products and services. Ideas build the world around us and how we want to interact with it.

Short-lived and practical, or grand and ambitious, we grab ideas every day, we mix our ideas with others, combining and making something big from such small beginnings. There is something truly magical about that ability.

This is a superpower you can hone, now

There are real, practical processes and tools you can employ. Tangible techniques to create and elevate an idea into something much more, and quickly.

Questions

How do you know the next big movie in the series from your favorite director will be great and take a billion dollars at the box office?

Why does a product launch from a technology company make global press and get thousands sleeping overnight outside the store?

What makes fans obsess over their favorite characters and their stories?

What makes them become advocates, walking billboards with their branded T-shirt?

Simply answered, underpinning all these successes, are repeatable creative processes using straightforward tools to generate, identify, scrutinize, develop and maximize ideas. Ideas that launch with a laser-like targeting on audience need.

The antithesis of fluid idea generation? No.

There is a set of tools in use here, *not* a set of instructions telling you what to make with them.

An 'idea alphabet', capable of making limitless words

For more than 20 years in the UK and US, I've been developing and evolving these processes. From the workshops I run, to the projects I lead. From TV shows and movies, toys and household goods, from big pharma to even bigger utility companies. The tools continue to be used and to succeed.

Large corporates and lengthy projects. Small, niche and personal work that needs new thinking. These processes work.

My goal here is to detail techniques, how they can be applied and what they can achieve. Use them in combination with each other or pick and choose. If you have a need for idea generation, development and delivery, you'll find a technique here that can be applied.

What to expect?

I'll share practical methods for every stage of an idea's development. Snappy tools to kick start the impossible project and clear ways of jump-starting a slowly accelerating and lengthy piece of work.

Straightforward steps to starting projects with a superpower of curiosity and wonder. An ability to see and combine, the opportunities to overlay parallel ideas and be the alchemist making a new potion.

In the middle of development, I'll demonstrate how you must have a fierce focus to move an idea on, and clear ways you can achieve this. Proven ways to unblock the road ahead. Processes to cut through to what's important. The clarity to focus on customer need when the noise of a project distorts the music you need to make.

Taking that clarity and building ideas step by step. An iterative approach of continuous improvement. Avoiding the paralysis of a singular obsessive idea that will never be ready.

And because anyone can start a project, but not everyone can finish one, I'll focus heavily on the key methods to sell an idea. Selling to your team, your boss, your customers, repeatedly.

Once launched, shared or delivered, then what? What becomes of our great ideas and how do we manage that newness we created, now that it is old? I'll detail the approach to take.

Our limitless words make powerful stories

Supporting all these tools, I'll share the importance of a clear and structured narrative in the journey of our ideas. Why do we need one? What does it achieve? What are the key components? How do we use them? Stories are key and that narrative begins to be constructed on day one of an idea.

Those stories support us and our ideas as we begin to showcase our thinking to others. With that comes feedback, amends, actions to alter course. How do we manage that? And more importantly, encourage the right feedback. Feedback can add additional layers of strength and new characters in a story that your audience will want to be part of. It makes an idea better

Powerful stories deliver winning ideas

Regardless of all the processes we may have, delivering a winning idea is our target. We often care little about our favorite director's creative journey or the processes they may have employed, it's the movie we yearn to watch. We must never forget that all the techniques along the path are there to deliver that idea and to deliver it well, so let's begin.

CHAPTER ONE

Script the Story You Want Them to Read

Day one, minute one. The most influential piece of advice I was given early in my career.

Always think of the outcome that you want to achieve on minute one of a project, a meeting or even at the start of a day.

What are you doing? Making a cake? Building a bridge? Writing a book? Running 100 meters? What are you doing?

There's a brutal focus to it. You know where you're going and what you'd like to achieve, so you stay anchored on that delivery in all you do. Before we start sparking new ideas and processes, this is the first piece of structure we need to build. It's the foundation.

There are variants of phrases that sum this idea up that you can use. Between them they've helped to sell millions of books, spawned a thousand corporate offsite courses (I've done lots of them), it's in far too many internet videos and Google searches, but to be honest it does deserve its place in chapter one of this book.

'Script the story you want them to read'. This is the phrase I made and use. It's built of simple, solid elements that make it flexible and effective;

COMMITMENT – We're penning a script here, writing it down.

NARRATIVE – We're building a story framework to invent within.

AUDIENCE – We're building something of value for others.

OBJECTIVE – We have a plan, an outcome.

4 simple ingredients to stir into our alchemy cauldron.

This phrase gives our idea generation focus but avoids a hard stop conclusion every time we use it. We're not delivering an end (which would be tough to define on day one) it's simply a story, much like a chapter in a larger book. It gets us off and running with a plan.

Ideas are always iterative, and the story here is too. We take our narrative from chapter one and build on it in chapter two as we introduce new thinking and deeper details.

In life, we never end one piece of thinking, forget all about it, then start from scratch on something new the next day. No. There's history and knowledge here that we build on and we should recycle and reuse it later as our story progresses.

Knowing where you're heading is key. Scale the stories as the idea develops. Thinking solely of that big finale too early can in turn make it difficult to begin in my experience. Start your script for your story and focus on the 4 simple ingredients.

Commitment

Commit it, write it down. This isn't some long descriptive piece of text, it is purely an outcome sentence or two, it solidifies the plan. Committing it to paper versus having it in mind adds an extra layer of definition, much like committing an agenda to paper for all to see in the meeting. Meetings without an agenda tend to get to the wrap up "any other business" rather quickly in my experience. Ideas without a written starting story meander quickly too and you can miss the important stuff.

Script the second chapter. This idea ladders up, ready for use at the next meeting/conversation/presentation. We build continuity and don't need to start again at chapter one. We feel like we're making some progress, which at the start of bigger projects can be a huge benefit.

Narrative

The linking to a 'story' with all its connotations of locations, actors and props is key and strings an idea together. Idea stories are everywhere; they inform innovators, designers, strategists, marketeers, retailers and consumers. Whilst you might not use 'story' in your everyday conversations when talking about the next mobile phone you'll buy or in deciding which grocery store to visit, you do use another word. Brand.

Brands are stories

Brands aren't logos, colored signs above the door or even a specific product. Brands are the story you read; they are the narrative. Their audience are characters in the story, they play on their stage (shops or places you see the brand), they use their props (products) and they ideally follow the script they've written (path to purchase).

Scripting a story and writing a narrative is building a brand, and we do that early. You're building more than one idea or product by building a brand. You're building a framework to support a collection of ideas.

As our stories and brands develop it becomes easier and easier to add depth and more ideas that fit within that narrative. Importantly, we also know what doesn't fit, what isn't part of our brand, or our story we want others to read.

And if that story isn't working, not being read? Rebrand. Tell another story.

Rebranding is about changing your story, not the color of your font.

Audience

Our story's actors are our audience and our focus. Understanding 'why' they need something comes first. Minute one. There may be a problem that needs a new solution or a need to do something better, faster or more cheaply. Why do they need your solution? Even before you decide <u>what</u> that solution is.

Only after the 'why' do we talk about 'what' they need.

We understand the problem they need an answer for, before we start selling a solution. Once we have that problem and need identified, we can use that as part of our script of a solution the audience will want to read. It's audience first, otherwise we're coming up with great ideas that no-one needs. So, not great ideas. More on identifying that critical 'why' later.

Objective

The 'what' our audience needs. When we'll deliver it. Objectives are never the process, or instructional. Objectives don't tell you how to get there, they simply keep you laser-focused on what's important, what your goal is, what success looks like, no matter what your idea is. The 'what' is ultimately your answer to the need you've identified.

The 4 ingredients of early structure can easily form the basis of a more defined brief. A 'brief' in this instance is a set of information built from your first ideas, simply built out further to easily communicate with others.

A great design or idea brief outlines objectives and should always be a starting point, it's a moment of clarity and focus without being restrictive. No executional steps here.

Briefs frame the freeform creative thinking that comes later. If there's a team involved in the project they should be involved in the brief creation. If you can't agree a brief, you won't agree or excel during the creative idea process. Again, agree at the beginning on the story you want them to read.

I write briefs for myself; they aren't beautifully crafted, multi-page affairs. They are simple fuller 'scripts' that allow me to keep focus on the stories when my creative ideas start to meander.

Our stories and briefs are a place to come back to, time and again. A supporting foundational structure that supports without the shackles of instructions.

New Ingredients

No shackles?

No specific moments of defined creation?

No timeline to its completion?

A brief or the story you've written to support it, isn't a project plan. There's no play by play actions to follow. Where do I start?

Our 4 ingredients in our script don't deliver that solution, so we need to add more...

Looking to a distant presentation or delivery of an idea? A far horizon with just a brief in your hand? This is daunting and I've been there.

The risk is high. A sluggish start and a scrambled finish delivering a weak idea. A project post-mortem that says you needed more time. Classic.

"work expands so as to fill the time available for its completion".

Cyril Northcote Parkinson, The Economist, London 1955

Parkinson's law is as right today as it was in 1955. You may have 3 weeks, for example, to come up with the idea in your brief, and that's how long it will take you. In your planning, you build out a framework of activities to do, teams you talk to, reviews to undertake. We fill that time.

Those moments where you meander, procrastinate, lack focus. You have the time to have those moments, until you haven't. Then you focus and get a job done, just.

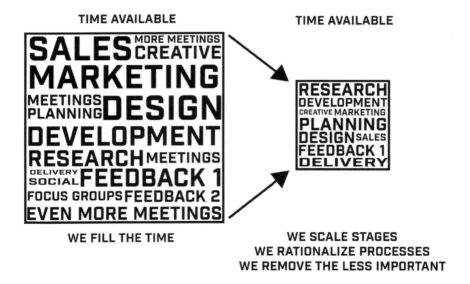

Let's cut those meandering moments out.

On our reduced plan we fill the time with the necessary, the important and needed.

3 weeks? Give yourself a day.

Let Parkinson's law work for you, now.

There's a great tool that's a key new ingredient we can use for this.

The one-day project.

In Brief

• Be clear on your objectives. A solid target is key to staying focused as you originate ideas organically. It is all too easy to lose sight of a tangible outcome in the flux of the new.

• Script the story you want them to read. Commitment, Audience, Narrative, Objective. Begin to shape a story for your idea using these 4 ingredients.

• Brands are stories your consumer experiences, not logos.

• Work expands to fill the time you give it. Give yourself less time. Use that shorter time to only focus on the important, the relevant and the need of your consumer.

CHAPTER TWO

Sprint

I've used the one-day project all my career. A fondness for it now – but terror, excitement, frantic work and rarely any time to think in the early days of its use.

The tool is clear – a brief is presented at 9:30 am. Final presentation to a group at 4pm same day. Finished.

Regardless of the end need of your project, big or small, set yourself one day to complete a related project. ONE DAY. If Parkinson's law is right, then you will complete the task given to you in that time.

You'll compromise time spent on the unnecessary.

You'll remove the stuff that doesn't answer the brief.

You'll stick to the brief like glue, you won't have time to meander or procrastinate.

Practically what do these 'one-dayer's' look like?

Firstly, identify WHY you need the 'one-dayer'. These three buckets of need might help refine and filter that.

The New Idea

You need something new. A new idea/product/process, where do you start with so many unknowns? You need a structure, a place to play, to create a myriad of fast ideas and to spark thinking to life.

Project Start

You've got a new big idea/project in development. There's a brief, it's a big project, lots of time. You need to jump start this project early. Give it some life, some rapid one-day idea generation that can spark bigger success later.

Mid Project

You are part-way through a larger project, and there are challenges. Somethings not right. We've hit an obstacle. Time is tight. The idea we have isn't working. We need to jolt the thinking we have, to test out something new, fast, low risk.

Once you have the 'why', that 9.30am brief should be more straightforward to write. We have the broad outcome clearly defined; we know what's needed, now we need details.

The brief is next to be outlined and whilst this will be unique to your situation, there are common techniques to help structure it as well as areas to avoid. This is how each of the three scenarios might translate.

The New Idea

The unknown

When a bigger project doesn't exist to connect to, there may be no obvious brief to twist or parallel path to create. Perhaps a simple corporate objective is communicated, a high-level financial goal or a market share target. Up to you to discover the solution.

Where do your ideas start?

The risks of wandering off directionless are high. No brief, no steering, no end to define or script.

One-day project? Yes. In seven or eight hours you'll have some ideas in the bank.

To start, there are always things we do know; the broad area of innovation, a tech space, a product for my company, a new way to reach customers etc.

Just that small start is enough to get going.

We can journey back to our consumer.

Who are they?

What else do they do?

What other innovation is going on in their world?

Where are they?

The one-day magic is to pose those bigger open questions. Overlay innovation going on elsewhere in our consumers world, add a spin and a twist. Flip the question. Change the sense. Climb one level up to keep it broad.

The tech question – "How do I get more visitors to my fashion website?", becomes the one-day "A customer is about to buy a garment in a bricks and mortar clothes store, what stops them?"

The product question – "What's next years must have toy?", becomes the one day "A family are in a driverless car, how do they play?"

We are laddering up on parallel innovations, well known and changing social patterns and focusing on consumer need.

We absorb future trends.

We become more curious, looking at the 'elemental'. Check out Chapter 6 for ways to do this.

We leverage the new ideas of parallel companies to ours that affect our consumers.

We look at the news all around us.

We use that latest app.

We build a story around all that information and plug our own ideas into it.

There's a lot we do know when we really listen to the surround sound blasting around our consumers. It builds our brief for our new idea.

Project Start

With all that time in front of you

Avoid making your one-day project the same as the larger project. This may seem counter intuitive, but this process is about thinking in a new way. Fast. Not getting bogged down or looking too far ahead.

Pick a theme for the brief that's parallel to, or with a twist on the bigger project. The likely outcomes of this are still relatable and translatable to the larger project but there's no baggage from it.

Think of your bigger project idea and change the scale, change the senses, change location. Take one step up the ladder from your specific larger project, the brief and the opportunities from it should be broader in scope.

Be open-ended on the output needed at the presentation at the end of the day.

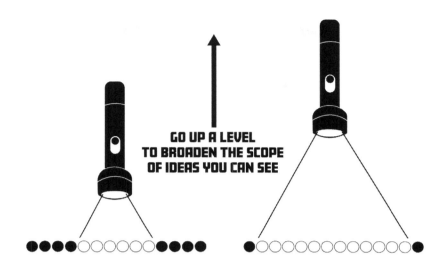

GO UP A LEVEL TO BROADEN THE SCOPE OF IDEAS YOU CAN SEE

Here's two examples of briefs;

Industry: Transport company

Larger Project: New vehicle model design

One day brief: "You're on a bus, what's missing?'

Much Q&A follows a brief like this...What? Part of the bus? The passengers? The posters? The scenery? The ticket? The Wi-Fi? Up to you, see you at 4 o'clock, is the answer, without sounding too flippant.

The open-ended deliverable could be a product or a service. It talks squarely to a need. It's missing, the consumer needs it. This is wholly about customer experience and could feed into an innovative feature for your bigger product launch.

The bus example is useful here for familiarity, simplicity and clarity. We have a very contained environment in which we can define so much. Whilst we may not all need to be creating in this niche business area, there are real parallels to a wide range of service industries.

Replace the 'bus' in the brief for another industry that provides a direct enclosed service for consumers. Hotels, shops, theme parks etc. The foundation of the question works across these and other businesses equally well.

We're broader, one rung up the ladder. This is not the specific 'You're on a bus, design me a new seat'.

This is idea thinking that's broad, with potential to focus later.

Avoid getting caught up in detail that can also steer outcome. Don't ask someone to design you a chair, design me something to sit on.

Fresher ideas come from a new place of reference, not the place you're at now. Take a step back. There are far too many 'knowns' in that chair example, it must have a back, 4 legs etc.

Something to sit on is a log, a brick wall, a carpet or...a plane. It's fresher thinking.

What if we take something less large and physical, more emotive, as an example of a brief?

Industry: Radio

Project: Rebrand (It's a new story, remember)

One day brief: "What do we look like?"

What? You mean sound like, right? What the logo? The radio station office? No, the 'station'. Capture what it delivers as an experience in a different medium. See you at 4 o'clock.

The open-ended brief talks about experience, it's about capturing an essence of your story, who your consumers are.

We all know radio stations sound different, the different genres and presenters. What if that audio personality extended into other mediums? Rebranding a radio station will involve all mediums and we need to refine that essence. We capture that story 'feel' which in turn informs the design work that comes later.

Any company or project that has a clear human sense (audio, touch, sight etc.) in its core delivery can use this method.

Questions

Canned drinks, how have they built a look and feel?

How does carbonated, flavored water translate into motor racing and extreme sports?

Why are holidays and a large red truck covered in lights so intertwined?

The answers? These are all about stories (brands) that translate from one sense to another. These brands captured the essence and flavor of one sense and overlaid it onto another. As those senses get broader, so does the appeal to your consumer. You're giving them more of what they need and like, in new ways. You're extending the brand.

Just be mindful of going too far, too soon. An extension, built on an extension...suddenly you're a long way from the core, the heart your consumer loved.

That consumer experience is key here.

How do customers feel about you?

Why do they like you?

What do they 'need' or expect from you?

We're reinforcing our story and our brand. The stuff that makes us gravitate to one company over another, that makes us queue to buy their tech products and buy their branded T-shirts.

Capturing human elements and having empathy with our consumers in any brief, one day or longer is key to the success of any new project.

Mid Project

With obstacles to smash

The need here is to break through an issue versus new thinking at the start of something larger.

The same rules still apply. Avoid a simple duplication of your larger project. That barrier is in your mind, move away from it when you have the chance.

Add a twist or mix it up by changing scale and sense etc. Take the step up one level and look there. A broader vista is fundamental here. Much like an obstacle in the road, we don't simply keep driving up to it and back again, hoping to get by. We find another way around.

Here's a brief for physical products;

Industry: Toys

Larger Project: New product launch

Obstacle: Pricing

One day brief: "What's important to our consumer?"

A pricing challenge is common. Prioritizing need for the consumer is the answer, the important stuff. We focus on consumers first, before we start looking for ways to cut cost. Be careful. The easiest piece to change to save cost might be the one reason your consumers buy your product.

In toys, cost reducing happens all the time. A must-have toy sits in front of you in the factory. Research tells us it must be a certain cost against competition, for retail to list it.

We've designed a 'Ferrari' in feature terms for the kids, but it needs to be priced as a 'Ford' for consumers to buy it. The approach is to focus on key needs from that toy for our consumer. We don't start on the quick-win price reductions.

Price reducing the fun out of a toy is bad. The easiest way to reduce 25% cost for a toy car is to remove a wheel. It just doesn't cut it.

Some more human-centered thinking is needed here. In one day, we can really cut through to that quickly, what's important to our consumer?

What are the elements to focus on? Cast the others away, reduce the cost and keep the fun.

How much can you take away and keep the idea and the amazing (important) features intact?

Taking the wheel off the car is too much, you're selling disappointment. There's a 25% cash saving elsewhere that comes at a far lower percentage cost to the experience and need of your consumer. Change the equation, change the cost without changing the desire.

There is also a valid alternative direction here. Is that obstacle really there? Is it truly impassable? We may be able to re-pitch and resell the premium-priced idea we have. Perhaps our consumers do need the 'Ferrari' after all. Can we demonstrate there's a real premium need that can support a premium solution? Match the premium 'why' of our consumer and the premium-priced solution of 'what' we deliver. One smashed obstacle.

Here's a brief for less physical products;

Industry: Publishing

Larger Project: New book launch

Obstacle: Finishing the Novel

One day brief: "The parallel story."

This is all about the conclusion of an idea.

How do we bring this thing to life?

How do I finish this story?

Again, an idea with a twist will help. Take a parallel path. You're heading in the same direction but on new ground.

Write a one-day short story, parallel themes to the larger novel. Mix up the place, the senses. No dwelling on the obstacle. Finish in one day.

You can take that skill and learning of wrapping up the narrative back to your novel. You've gained new ideas too. New content to put online before your bestseller book tour? A start on your next book in the series?

This is about experiencing the complete process of an idea from creation to a launch, learning how to win.

Second time is always easier than first. It's familiar to you as you transpose the learnings back to your bigger project.

Elite sports use this technique. Taking a proven, repeatable, winning solution back to a problem.

The routines of a kicker placing the ball.

The same set number of steps back and to the side.

The same glance at the ball, then the target.

Visualizing the run.

Targeting the precise location on the ball to make contact.

Tracing the ball's path between the posts.

In front of 50,000 fans, it's repeating the success you've already learned. When you finally kick it, you've got experience already of scoring, you know how to do it.

In Brief

• 9.30 – 4pm. It's a wonderfully creative day. Plan and make time for it and you'll be amazed at the results.

• Identify the needs of the day and craft a brief.

• New idea – Pin down what you do know. What are your customers experiencing elsewhere? Translate that parallel innovation back to your world.

• Project start – Twist the bigger project you have. Make the project broader and always focused on consumer need.

• Mid project – Take a parallel path with a complete conclusion in a day. Visualize that total completion and bring the result back to the obstacle you face.

CHAPTER THREE

One Powerful Day

Our brief is set, now to the practicalities. Your industry, company or team are unique but there are common methods that can work for all.

Tell the team this one-day project is coming a few days out.

Ensure the day is blocked, meetings cleared. No calls to 'hop-on' later.

Don't tell them the brief. The same goes if you're setting yourself a one-day project. You'll know the brief of course, but don't start thinking about it before the day. Give yourself the same constraints, the same opportunities for new thinking.

If you are working with a larger group, there are some key points to consider;

>•Keep the teams tight, maximum six people. Everyone needs to participate and larger teams just fragment.

>•Mix up skills and background to gain a diversity of approach. A group of six engineers may have the same education and approach to a problem, the same blind spots.

>•Mix up ages and levels.

This last point can be massively important with any kind of idea generation that includes technology or social media. Why?

Ensure your youngest participants are dispersed amongst your groups. That emerging social media platform that you've never heard of. They use it all the time.

That app, that way of using a certain technology. Make sure the understanding of that is peppered amongst those with other skills and experience.

You may have been on a training course about that new tech. You may think you know about it. You don't. The people who use it every day in their normal lives know it better, and importantly, they know the other brands and their stories are on it. As a minimum, get those individuals to give an overview to the wider group before you start, if there's not enough of them to be planted in each team.

9.30am

The day begins.

Get the basics done – share who's in each team. Get some pens and pads and space for each group. Introduce the idea of the day and the deadline.

Share the brief - outline the plan and objective.

What's needed at 4pm? A 5-minute team presentation outlining the idea, the benefits etc. What does it look like? How do you deliver it? A complete colored-in story.

It should be enough of a narrative to withstand 5 minutes of peer Q&A.

Presentations should be in a recordable format – screen, sketches, interpretive dance (just video it), Q&A from the audience.

Make sure you get all the presentations done in an hour at the end of the day, so adapt team sizes and timings to suit. Any longer and you've lost the crowd.

Then present the brief and answer any questions, but don't steer output.

During the day and especially early on, questions will come up as teams grapple with the brief. Keeping the topic broad is the key. If we're on our bus (or another enclosed service example), we can remind teams to think about:

The whole experience.

Put themselves in that environment.

Who's there?

What else is going on?

What are they doing?

Where are they going?

What happens when X or Y happens?

The teams can organize themselves and how they may want to divide up roles. They can also decide on what idea generation techniques throughout the day they choose to deploy. More on those later.

4.00pm

At four pm, the mad rush ends as per Parkinson's law and presentations begin, a myriad of mixed thinking.

There's no right or wrong, they'll be common ground and random thoughts, some more fantastical than others.

Across the room there has been a laser targeted focus for a sharp period on key idea generation. The key is to utilize that amazing set of assets.

Record all the presentations, keep the power points, flip charts and dance videos. Jot down the questions and answers that are raised.

Get a smaller group together the next day – one from each team and leadership perhaps, to go through the output again. This isn't simply a recap or a sharing of the process. With more senior team feedback, ensure this is an edit, a tighter evaluation and the defining of a concrete path to actioning great ideas and demonstrating tangible outcomes. It's demonstrating a vision with a route to execution.

Identify and distil the gems, the ideas that sparked a bigger idea for a new project or solved that impasse or ignited a new idea or area to explore. It'll amaze you how many times that stack of great thinking will be referred to in the future.

The good news is you can do these one-day projects at any time when some new and quick thinking is required. They don't need to be massive undertakings with every team involved either, they can flex in scale easily. As to the reaction in teams...some will hate the process, the disorder, the open-ended structure, the 'waste' of time.

Others will love the craziness, but all will look back at something tangible that was born, developed and presented in a day. It may not be the end idea that people will remember, it might a comment that came up in the presentation or an idea that you rejected at 9.45am in the flurry of panic. Those moments can stick and short-circuit a bigger idea or something sparky could create a new parallel project.

The forced complete progress of a project in totality moves on your thinking. It delivers the whole process and flags potentially tough moments ahead on a larger project. It mixes up what may have been presented as a very linear, step by step process reaching far into the distance.

No matter the length of your typical projects, you don't normally expect to be presenting a final idea to a group on day one. But doing so is a good thing.

In Brief

• Build mixed teams. Mixed ages, abilities, skills and talents.

• Pay special attention to tech innovation. Share your youngest team members across the groups. There is huge equity and benefit in their day-to-day technology usage.

• Present the brief, but don't steer conclusions. A little chaos and lack of definition is a good thing. The focus is clearly on solving the brief and not on predetermined ideas.

• Capture it all. Record the presentations, photograph the work sheets. Encourage feedback on the process from the teams.

CHAPTER FOUR

94.3% of Statistics Are Made Up*

*Including this

We need (good) data. As we start to put in place the one-day projects and begin igniting our idea thinking, we need info.

It's likely your brief might be anchored by data, the solid irrefutable insights that have identified a need and an opportunity. Senior teams may demand (and expect) stats, in order to believe your ideas are real and to demonstrate a market exists.

When we're thinking about our consumers, there is a clear need to understand them. We must understand 'why' they need us and our ideas and therefore 'what' we can deliver.

We in turn need the data to steer our ideas for our briefs and one day projects. Who are they? What do they do? Why do they do it? Where are they?

All this great info informs those briefs, the budgets and the approach we take in idea generation. Foundational information that tells us where to fish, what the fish like to eat, that sort of thing.

We just need the ideas on the right fishing equipment to use. Straightforward.

Nothing brings all this info on a consumer to life like a consumer profile. Let's make the consumer real, an identity and a persona filled with all the choices they would make.

Sophie

I've seen profiles developed to an amazing depth on the ideal consumer for an idea – She's 28, called Sophie, Married, 1 child, holidays twice a year, donates to charity etc. We are creating ideas for her, so let's ask her what she wants.

We can ask our audience what the 'answer' is, but do they know, and should we trust them anyway? Do they do (and buy), as they say they do?

They are grounded in their current world of reality and of their perceived reality. Perceived reality?

Perceived reality is simply the perception of who our consumer wants to be and the therefore the persona they portray. Sophie does yoga, loves a smashed avocado, small dogs and composts her ground Ecuadorian coffee according to her social media pages. She'd never visit a burger joint, or so she said in the research.

There has always been a level of portraying the 'right image' in our public profiles. Keeping up with the neighbors.

It's just that our neighborhoods are growing.

In 2012, the average person had 3 social media accounts, in 2019 they had 8.3 accounts each *

*not made up

We can ask all the right questions in the right way, but our audience can be great storytellers, Instagram's short-term updates even encourage it by labelling them as stories.

"I wonder what this researcher really wants me to say?"

"I wonder what the 'right' answer is?"

"What would social media Sophie say?"

There's a lot of consideration and work that goes into building out the correct pubic profile on those 8+ accounts.

Even kids without the social media persona do the same. Take some of the preschool TV shows I've worked on. Kids loved the show and wanted the T-shirt and so we sold great looking garments to kids up to about the age of 5 (just as they start school). After that, the T-shirt and brand isn't cool on the playground currency market. "I'm not advocating that 'baby' brand by wearing that T-shirt near my friends" they'd infer. Nothing wrong with that you'd say, they've simply outgrown the brand. Except we continued to sell a good number of pajamas to 8-year-old kids for the same brand.

Simply, these kids liked the brand enough to want a product until they were 8 in the privacy of their own home.

Would they go outside where their friends might see them aged 6? No.

In a focus group; "Do you like the brand?" No.

If we'd listened to that (or the retailer buyers heard that) in research, we'd all have missed several years of sales of certain products. We would have not delivered what the consumer wanted and not put money in the bank.

Before the research and insights leaders reading this book demand a refund and leave a scathing review online, I am in no way reducing the validity and necessity for great data driven info and for those whose skills isolate the music from the noise. Indeed, there is an immense craft to getting great quality information and interpreting and building robust analytics to inform direction. In an age where anyone can extract 'data' from almost any online source, the need for heightened scrutiny and the craft of the insight's teams on the interpretation of it only intensifies.

Research group meetings are intriguing to watch.

We're huddled behind a mirrored screen, like in all the best police dramas. The group are in the room, glancing across towards us occasionally. I don't *think* they can see us...

We watch the dynamics of a group.

We observe the flow of questioning.

Our bolder consumers leading the charge, making sure their persona is aspirational or 'right' in the eyes of the others.

We see emerging leaders of the panel driving the feedback.

Sophie says she would never visit a burger joint and all the others nod. So, 100% of our consumers never visit a burger joint.

Done. Data.

We have so many tools to collect data to inform our ideas now. We can ask direct questions so easily now through a variety of media to just the right person (or the right profile). We openly and frequently share our likes, habits and purchases more passively with online data.

I get in my car and my phone tells me how long it will take to get to work. I've 'told it' through habit at this certain time I leave this location and go to that place. As it's that time and I'm in my car, it's got a fair idea that's where I'm going now. Such amazing (some may say scary) data is accessible and from it we can build a great picture of who we maybe creating ideas for and their needs.

What this data tells us though is the current, the existing processes, places and products our consumer's experience. Any ideas we may create would fit into this current world.

We know Sophie (poor Sophie is getting picked on) likes to purchase certain products online. The algorithm for the store tells her she would also like a related product. It just so happens the store has an offer on that the day she views it.

The store can never say that what she'd really like (or more importantly, need) is something they don't sell or that hasn't been made yet.

In parallel, my phone data says I need a new app to find a faster route into the office. There's one available too, by chance.

The offer vs. the need

The 'offer' here is simply a product or service that is available now and that app is selling it. The same app will never (and can't) talk about what I need. It will never say there's a great idea needed so that my job can be done from home. The data is selling and reinforcing what's on offer (the faster route to the office with a new app) and not what I need (the way I can work from home). More on that later.

We of course will find gaps or consumer struggles and nuggets of great info in all our data pieced together.

We must evaluate it though, to inspect it, to scrutinize it and to do all this with new idea thinking. It can be all too easy to present data as absolute fact, as definitive and right, superseding all else. Final.

In a head to head presentation, data will always beat 'just an idea', it's measurable and fact. Just make sure it truly is that robust.

Data can be easy to hide behind too if the worst happens.

"We made a loss this quarter, sold a third fewer new products. The data said we should have sold more, and the focus group loved them". Excellent, that makes that ok then.

Well done all, we followed the data. It's unlikely though your bonus is based on selling fewer products.

Data is a valuable tool to add to the mix just like all the creative generation processes we have in this book.

We use data to learn, inform and shape a direction. We interpret it and unleash our imagination and intuition to amplify the ideas behind it all to truly innovate. When we build something big, new and innovative, just make sure the bricks of information we use are strong enough.

In Brief

• In a world of easy desktop research, increase your scrutiny of the information that may be presented as definitive. Your idea is too important to be built on poor foundations.

• Understand people personas and the increasing challenge of perceived realities in social media and beyond.

• Digital data records the current and delivers solutions based on available supply, not on need.

• Data is not an outcome. It is a means to endorse decisions that shape a successful product. It's the successful product we sell, not the approach we took to get there. Always take the path to deliver a great solution, not the one that simply supports the data.

• In a sea of data, avoid only looking for, or only selecting, information that backs your current hypothesis.

CHAPTER FIVE

Creating is hard, editing is easy

One winning idea at the end of rainbow. In those spacious weeks of longer projects, it's easy to get caught up looking for treasure. That definitive golden idea. You're searching for it, perfectly presented in a box and ready to go. Any other idea you walk past on that hunt is just not going to make it, there's the ultimate new idea just over there and I'm going to get it, come what may.

Looking for the one idea, the absolute answer and the clear winner is risky. You can spend far too much time rejecting or not even evaluating good ideas and never find that champion.

How will you even know when you do find it?

Chances are it won't be presented beautifully in a treasure chest and there might be another one just under the next rainbow.

When do you stop looking?

Total paralysis, it's the golden idea or nothing, and there's a high chance it'll be nothing.

We can help ourselves out here by lowering our expectations to start with then incrementally increasing them.

What!? This is about making the best idea we can!

Finding treasure is tough

Creating that one amazing idea in totality and ready to go is not just risky, it's tough. Taking a good idea and refining it is more straightforward. This process doesn't rely on the luck of a single rainbow discovery, it focuses on iterations of constant improvement. There's never a flashing sign above the idea you should choose.

Ask a group of people to come up with a definitive idea for a new app and you'll struggle to find the treasure. Show the same people an app design or other idea in progress and get them to comment on it. They can edit and you'll move on the idea and make it better. It's simply easier to edit something in front of us than to originate. You can ask a lot more people to help you out too.

Everybody edits every day; we see things we don't like, and we comment.

Whether it's in broad terms or specific, there is an ease in commenting and editing, versus the tough creation part.

So, what's the plan here? Get an idea out there. You know it's got the potential to be treasure, but it needs work to be truly golden.

The key challenge is taking those comments, figuring out the fix and putting it into tangible and actionable steps.

It's all well and good receiving comments to elevate an idea, but there needs to be a step; "I know what's wrong (from the comments), and I know how to fix it (skill)".

You're not going to get the fix from your comments necessarily, you'd be asking a lot from your editor, but they'll certainly tell you what doesn't work.

A lot more on feedback and the edit of ideas later, but the key point here is about the early stage of idea creation.

Don't get paralyzed by only hunting for the perfect

In the same way our one-day projects jolted our thinking, the approach here is to focus on raw idea creation. Don't get bogged down in the details.

Ignore your inner voice or the neighbor voice of your colleagues finding obstacles or issues with your ideas just as they emerge. Ideas will have flaws and problems that need a fix, but they have potential with fixes to be great.

Don't use obstacles as reasons to throw an idea away too early. "It's not perfect now so we'll drop that idea." That kind of thinking simply results in good ideas never having the chance to be great, it's such a waste of potential.

Invention or Innovation?

There's a clear difference here.

Invention is a brand-new solution to a problem. It's rare and tough to find. The *first* of its kind.

Innovation is the iterative. It's a new way, a better way, of doing something that can be done already. We have a head start if we innovate on the invention of the past and we should always be open to this.

Remove the bad and replace with the good.

Take the good and make it better.

The number one selling vacuum cleaner, the number one selling phone, the number one selling car. All three aren't made by the companies that invented the originals. Today's market leaders didn't invent. They innovated.

They didn't get caught up only looking for the definitive new invention.

The reverse of all of this can be equally bad. Believing the answer you have is the definitive idea in the chest at the end of the rainbow.

"What I have doesn't need an edit and I won't hear a word against it."

We all get too precious sometimes. My first attempt at throwing a bowl on a potter's wheel bought that home to me. I thought my slightly wobbly creation was great. Ceramic course complete.

My tutor simply said, "Don't be too precious with your pots". Reluctantly I scraped it off the wheel, got new clay and made a better one. It's the continual development of ideas, appraising and building on the old with feedback and delivering the new. The ideas and skills learned from that first one informed the second.

Idea iteration is in your pocket

When was the last time that app on your phone was updated, or that operating system?

Simply, that was a good idea being updated to a better one.

Your operating system on your computer didn't start on version 10.1, it started on version one and it has been made incrementally better ever since.

That process is an idea being edited. Issues were found by a group of users telling the tech company the problems, they edited the idea and the team knew how to fix them. Update.

The tech company didn't attempt to design every feature the software has now from day one, it would have never launched. The world moved on. New technologies dropped in. Faults were found, but ultimately a strong idea wasn't paralyzed by the desire of perfection on day one.

We respect that process as consumers. Companies who continually strive to give consumer's the best products and are continually investing in updates to achieve that. We bought a product at version one but we're getting a new and improved product at version three.

Question

Good product now, then better one every year,

Or

No product now and version three in a few years?

Most consumers would go for the former. Indeed, there's no guarantee version three would be as good anyway without those early years of customer feedback.

Create & Update

It might be a tech-firm phrase, but 'beta' testing is a great idea we can all use. It's also everywhere even if you don't spot it. The idea is simple - we launch something not final and get feedback.

It's a great way of flagging to a consumer that what they're looking at;

Has potential

Isn't complete

Welcomes edits

There is also a big piece of brand trust here. I'm engaging fans, those loyal buyers, I'm demonstrating I want them to be part of the brand as it develops. They are helping write the next (successful) chapter in the brand narrative.

The idea of 'create and update' was reinforced to me recently when I bought a games console and a game on a disc.

I set up the machine, unwrapped the game box and inserted the disk...update required. Not a game had been played.

Not just a small, 'we've tweaked this problem' update...no, this was fundamental. Gigabytes of data, I was downloading a whole new version of the game I had bought on the disk.

Here, the processes of the physical and digital collide.

The game on my disk I bought was good and complete when they made the disks some months ago. The disks were made, boxes printed, shipped for weeks from the factory to the warehouse and on to the store.

Had I entered the store and bought the game? No.

I entered the store and bought a key to unlock a new game.

The disk manufacturing and shipping allowed more editing and creation by the games company. The physical/digital collision was a process opportunity for them to iterate a better idea. When I put the disk in, it triggered the latest version of the idea to be downloaded from the company. If they had waited to find the 'treasure' of version two and then manufactured the disks and shipped, they would have lost months of sales.

This collision of worlds is temporary

Years ago, we bought disks and their updates were slow and limited in scope by our internet speed. Our business models and teams delivered large, infrequent products. Bill Gates, on stage, launching a new Windows version on CD every couple of years. We are in the phase where no one will need the disk.

In 2019, more than 80% of video games were sold in a digital format

Time is ebbing away for physical formats. I was one of the diminishing 20% still buying a disk. But change the delivery and you change the game for those whose ideas <u>can</u> be digital.

Ultimately, it's now create, update, update, update.

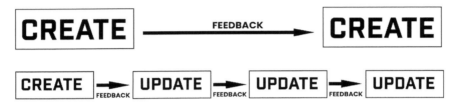

There's no need to wait months to get products into your consumer's hands anymore.

A new digital product can be updated and delivered multiple times in a day. No use for those boats delivering the physical formats.

Beta is no longer a stage before that big delivery, it's an ongoing state for many teams and companies. Version numbers now have lots of decimal points after them.

As consumers we've got used to this approach too, giving constant reviews and feedback. We're far more open and familiar with those version numbers and iterations. A change driven here in tech, may open new possibilities elsewhere.

Possibilities to generate great ideas, to deliver and to update them frequently. The need to search for definitive treasure is reducing daily.

In Brief

• Looking for a perfect, definitive solution and never launching an idea is bad.

• Change your launch process to be frequent and iterative. Adapt to accept new technologies and the consumers openness to update, update, update.

• Engage your consumers. Give them a beta, a test product they are willing to make better for you.

• Don't be precious with ideas. Every idea can be improved. No exceptions.

CHAPTER SIX

Be Curious

They all exist already. Ideas are elemental, made of chunks that make other ideas and everything else around us. This is the ideas alphabet we introduced earlier, capable of making unlimited words. Simply unique combinations of small elemental pieces.

Moving this to a practical level, you can take steps back from any innovation and you can trace a path to the familiar and the known, the current, the elemental base letters. What we see in innovation is a unique combination of these elements, treated, twisted and combined in new ways.

This concept is liberating. You may think it's too lofty and abstract though, so let me get into the details.

We all have the potential to mix up something new and the ingredients to do that are all around us already.

Observe an idea, translate it to your world, change it, adapt it, add another idea in the mix, change the scale, how you use it.

Boom. Innovation.

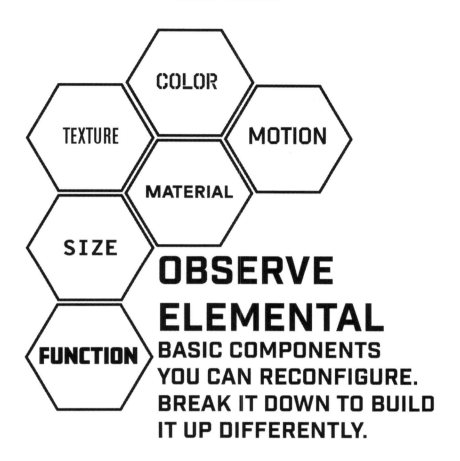

OBSERVE ELEMENTAL BASIC COMPONENTS YOU CAN RECONFIGURE. BREAK IT DOWN TO BUILD IT UP DIFFERENTLY.

This is an idea superpower I call morphing.

We start with one idea, one detail, one elemental observation, and layer on change, change, change, to get something new.

You can use it right now, part of a structured idea creation session, like a one-day project, or in isolation.

Sense check

We are all inherently curious. We all have powers of critical observation. Observation is more than looking. We don't just see, we review details, materials, function. We analyze like an artist.

What makes that thing beautiful?

What's it made of?

How does it fit with other things around it?

How does that work?

Look out of your nearest window, the city, your garden. Look big at skylines, look small at leaves. Observe individual people, or group interactions.

Walk out the door, take a sense check. Not some common-sense critique. In a real way, check all your senses. The smell, the sights around, the colors, the noises, the feel of what you're standing on, the temperature. Analyze that moment.

Observe the everyday to create the extraordinary

That kingfisher bird by your local river that dives into water silently, catching unsuspecting fish below.

Scale and morph. Bullet trains in Japan have their noses modelled on the kingfisher's beak to reduce noise as it travels. The train also travels 10% faster now.

The 2008 Olympic pool, full of swimmers wearing shark skin inspired swimsuits. The small textured areas on a shark's skin were shown to produce low pressure areas, less drag. Take that idea, synthesize it, adapt it, morph it. Create a new idea, a new swimsuit. Win.

Such suits have since been banned in the Olympics...

There are numerous examples of biomimicry like this. Copying and being inspired by nature's technology and applying to a human challenge.

We can also look at parallel human achievements.

The crafted Samurai sword, with unique manufacturing processes, using immensely strong and thin metal; inspiration for the design and engineering of Apple's iPad.

More than just physical design, we can observe and morph ideas across any discipline. Look for great ideas in other businesses, environments and mediums and translate and morph to yours.

Morphing tools

Morphing can work in 2 ways.

1)We can begin with our problem – we need a faster swimsuit.

2)We can begin with an observation – that shark swims fast and I found out why.

1)Let's start with our swimsuit problem. We have a clear environment and objective. We're in the water, at speed, and we want to go faster.

Take an easy and obvious parallel, what else goes fast in water? Animals, boats, sound? Then switch on the observation. Research papers written on each, personal analysis, individual watching and learning. Those swimsuit designers weren't shark experts to start with.

Is it shape? Is it material? Temperature? Texture?

Why? Get the detail. We're not going to literally take a shark skin and sew it into a swimsuit shape as it is. Distil the important stuff, get back to those elemental idea alphabet letters. What makes it work? Then we transpose back to our problem. We can squash and scale it to human size, adapt it to our shape, morph the idea of shark speed into human speed. Win.

Observation builds innovation

2)We start from an observation. We have something of clear interest, a big benefit, some fast shark 'technology'.

Where could I take this tech? Where else is it applicable? A new business venture, innovation beyond the sea or pool. Think of our one-day project for the new project without the brief, we observed what was going on in our consumers lives and their needs. Here we've observed a solution to a need.

Whose need?

Why do they need this?

What will it achieve?

We've therefore identified a great idea and a real demand. We then employ our morphing tools, scaling, adapting and twisting the idea. If we stay in the sea, a new paint finish for faster boat hulls? We move to other places where we get water, glass coverings that allow water and dirt to run off windows more quickly? Win. Rain jackets, washing machine components, we have options for water innovation everywhere.

There are times when we don't have an immediate clear need. We are building a broad idea bank. Throughout our lives we've added to this; school, work, family, travel, all adding new ideas. When a problem presents itself, we can draw from that, or at least have initial knowledge to go and investigate more deeply. I remember something about shark skin being fast, let me find out more.

Adding to that idea bank is something we can all do easily. Observe, record and always be curious.

Take that curiosity and play with morphing tools.

  •Play with scale. What happens if that concept was big or tiny? How does it change use, does it unlock something new?

  •Overlay human need. What would a human gain by being able to use that idea? What do I need to do to make it work for us?

  •Change material. If that idea could be made of something else, we could do so much more. How can you make that happen?

•Change location and medium. Take a whale fin out of the water. Transpose its bumps and scalloped edges and you can make a wind turbine with blades that gather more energy.

•Multiply. One of a good idea is great. What happens if you had multiples of the same idea? One dot, one pixel on a TV screen emits a single beam of light, hundreds give you the opportunity to make images.

These actions and more can be overlaid again and again in unique combinations. Straightforward ideas, simply observed, innovatively morphed.

In Brief

• All ideas are elemental. They can be broken into pieces, reconfigured and adapted into the new.

• Truly observe in detail. Check your senses, the big vistas and the smallest landscapes. Take what you see and adapt and transpose to a new scale or sense.

• Nature delivers amazing solutions that are applicable beyond the observed application.

• There are amazing techniques and processes in other industries. Could these be applied to your idea?

• Build idea banks ready to use in the future.

• Morphing tools are powerful. Twist, scale, multiple and apply to elements to generate new ideas.

CHAPTER SEVEN

Creative-ideation-ery-maps

Buzzword Bingo. At the office, there's excited talk of 'disruptive and bleeding edge' processes for generating new ideas.

"We're 'ideating' this week."

"We'll 'mind map' the 'brain dump' we started on Tuesday."

Sounds all very creative and very 'now'. The latest in idea 'technology' and so much better than last year's processes, we're told.

I'll just call the terms in this corporate speak a 'brainstorm' for simplicity. I'd encourage you to carry that simplicity into the methods you deploy.

Whilst the terms are as varied as the techniques used, the basic principal of isolating some time to generate ideas is constant.

Real innovation can come from them.

Trendy brainstorm processes come and go. The desire to roll dice for more and more random thoughts. Each method pushing everyone to 'think out of the box', to squeeze the maximum amount of ideas out of everyone in increasingly abstract ways.

A method to create artificial problems to then solve. We have that.

A process to force everyone in turn to speak no matter what they have to say. You will have a contribution, like it or not. Yep, got that too.

There will be advocates for these new 'must-use' approaches and you may already have another technique that you find works for you. That's the key point, it needs to work for you. With complexity of process comes rules to learn.

There's no such thing as a bad idea

You've heard it before no doubt. Unfortunately, it's wrong. Bad ideas tend to arrive more frequently from bad brainstorms. The way to keep generating good ideas is to keep the objective as a clear focus. Poor ideas emerge more regularly when a brainstorm is too broad, or the process hasn't been clearly defined. Loads of random ideas flying around, off-topic and tricky to manage as they spiral out of control.

The principal here is that a brainstorm is open and ideas show be free flowing, but within some structure. Structure gives us direction without stalling our flow of great ideas.

Good brainstorms, those with clear structure and an objective, will deliver great ideas.

Time to learn the rules is time not playing the game

I'd simply share that I've seen the best results from the most straightforward ways of brainstorming.

You may be remembering that terrible brainstorm. It ate into your day and nothing good came from it. It's easy to say "we're having a brainstorm" without really setting it up to maximize its effectiveness.

Get some structure. Lay some guidelines. Get those repeatable creative processes in place.

This is us using our idea alphabet, to create limitless words.

Like our design brief and our story chapters we script, there needs be an objective we intend to deliver to keep us focused.

Like our brief we're not detailing the specifics of outcome.

We want to be open to parallel ideas that can be transplanted back to our need, just like our one-day project.

There's a need to detail the practicalities of a brainstorm, not everyone has done them before, or at least the way you run them. Some people are scared by the last one they did and enter this one with a dose of skepticism, and their phone, to check emails.

If your participants don't know the (simple) rules, they can't play the game. "I wasn't sure if today was the right time to share this great idea I've got" is not something you want to hear in the bar after the event.

The size of a brainstorm can vary massively, but the rules and objectives are the same. As an example, in your one-day project you may have a brainstorm which could be a snappy sixty minutes. I've been to brainstorms events that last two days and involve more than eighty people so it's a flexi tool.

Have an objective overall for the one team or many – This is what we're here to do everyone, and why we're doing it.

"We need next year's product line as our customers don't like the products we've got now" for example.

Give each team an area to focus on. This is the piece of the objective for each. Team A get this product category. Team B could get the same or a different one, depending on how big the category is.

There are brainstorm variants (of course there are) where teams sequentially inherit and build on another team's ideas but keep it simple to start with.

Give each team the rules of the game – this is the structure of the brainstorm session, the timings, the expectations and the tools they must play with.

On to practicalities...

People

The power truly comes in getting people together. Where I've seen the best results are in groups of no more than six people in a team.

Enough heads to get a range of ideas and good amplifying of other's ideas (more on that later). It's not so many that there's little room for everyone to contribute. Team of ten? You'd lose at least a third of them to silence or their phones.

In reality it's six plus one. The seventh is the moderator, the chairman, the questioner, the juicer and the scribe.

The seventh doesn't need to know much about the topic. It can be beneficial if they don't. They could be external to the company. Their role is to get the ideas out of the others with the classic big open questions and starting thoughts.

Why are your customers rejecting this year's product?

What could we do about it?

You say we could make a new app. Tell me more about it, what does it do?

The moderator is there to encourage new thoughts and to encourage excavation more deeply into ideas that are discovered.

Like our one-day teams, the six should have a mix of skills and roles, backgrounds and ages. As a reminder this is about building mixed points of view whilst eliminating blind spots and splitting those up who have similar approaches to problem solving.

Place

Lift the brainstorm process away from distractions.

It doesn't need to be at an exotic 'off-site' location, just away from the normal day or the normal places the team frequent. That meeting room you always use? Use somewhere else. This is about framing the idea that this brainstorm is about the new, with no baggage of the now.

Depending on the scale of the brainstorm there may be other teams of six (seven) in other rooms or places. You shouldn't be able to see or hear them. My eighty-person brainstorm? We had small groups in multiple locations in the building.

Props

The seventh is the guardian of some sticky flip charts or large sticky pads, some colored pens and colored stickers.

The six just bring their brains, a pen and few regular sheets of white paper. Their phones are off, their regular notebooks or tablets closed.

 Everything gets written on the flip chart by our scribe. If the six need to jot themselves notes to bring up later they can do so on the paper, which is collated at the end of the day. We'll collect everything later, hence no notes in notebooks.

Time

After an hour, you'll lose people and their enthusiasm. With my two-day brainstorm, we did multiple sessions of one hour each per day, the rest was the supporting surround sound (more on that shortly).

This time could be compressed, and a smaller group could spend less time too, but don't go longer. If you have eight people, set up two teams, don't be tempted to do one larger and longer session.

The 5 & 25 Plan

The less the process feels contrived and artificial, the more accessible, straightforward and focused the idea generation will be.

No points for following the process perfectly but getting no great ideas.

We have an hour, a clear, solid breakdown of a plan looks like this:

INTRO

•5 MINUTES
•The moderator explains the objective and what we're brainstorming.

IDEATE

•25 MINUTES
•The teams work through ideas with the moderator probing and questioning the ideas as they emerge, then writing down the ideas on the board.

INTEROGATE

•5 MINUTES
•The team choose their top three ideas. Everyone adds stickers to their individual top three. Top three stickered ideas win.

INTERPRET

•25 MINUTES
•Three Ideas are divided amongst the team to develop further. Each mini team refines their idea and develops a 'movie poster' formatted page to pitch it.

Fewer than 6 on a team? Reconfigure the number of ideas selected to interpret. No teams of one. The seventh is there to support and help the mini teams as they develop the ideas.

Our Idea, 'The Movie'

The 'movie poster' format we develop in the interpret phase has one simple objective; quickly sell the idea you've created and refined.

When we come to pitch our idea to others, we have a clear layout. Use big flip chart paper. Like on all good movie posters, we include key pieces of info to inform our audience of the story we're telling.

Identity

Give your idea a name. It needs to be remembered. Add your team name and the topic too.

Bullet

Why and what does this idea deliver? Bold bullets headlining why the idea is needed. Nobody reads the small text at the bottom of a movie poster. These larger notes will help guide you as you present the idea later.

Visualize

Capture the spirit of the idea in an image wherever you can. A simple sketch, a diagram or a plan.

Annotate

Bring that visual to life, how it works, what it does.

Consistent design with this type of key info and idea clarity is a great thing. In twenty-five minutes, an idea movie poster gets formatted like this:

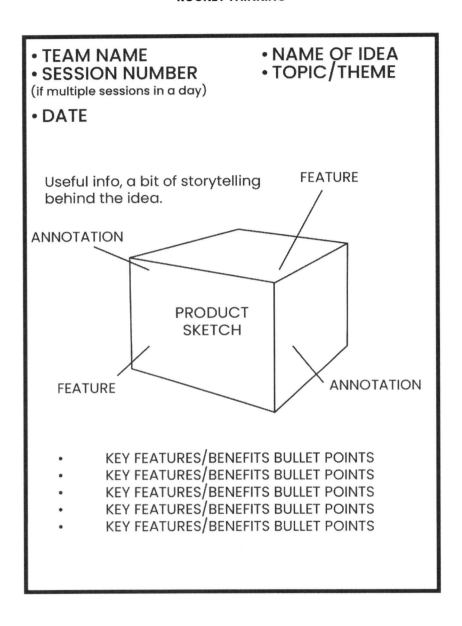

To help visualize the brainstorm process and the movie poster further, I've included more on this in the free idea generation pack you can download at: www.AndrewWoolnough.com/PBFree

An hour is done, we have our movie poster. Parkinson's law has ensured we're completed in time.

We head back to meet up with the rest of the groups, each holding their 'movie posters' of their three best ideas.

Pitch

Up on a big shared wall go the posters, clear for all to see. One by one, each mini team presents their ideas. The remaining members of the six who brainstormed together can of course contribute as they were there when the idea was born, but the focus is on those who developed it.

Five minutes per idea should be enough to sell it.

Once complete, the whole group votes on the ideas. Each person adds a colored sticker on their three favorite ideas. The posters, given our layout directions are clear and informative. This clarity helps everyone remember the idea that was just pitched.

You'll see similar ideas splitting the vote, one or two stand out winners (they tend to be 'sticker magnets' once they get a few votes) and some with no votes.

All the movie posters and the original ideate pages are collected and photographed. Record everything, there could be great ideas in those initial sparky sheets of ideas that didn't get refined.

All the pages, and any others from other brainstorms sessions in the day, can be pulled together and shared with the team easily now they're digital.

As with the one-day projects, pages should be reviewed the next day by a smaller team to work out the next steps to develop. Just don't have a brainstorm without the follow up and review. If (and when) one of those ideas truly develops and grows, make sure to always shout loud where it started. Brainstorms can get bad press sometimes, celebrate the process when it works well.

This has been a single block of a brainstorm, made of two parts, the one-hour team phase followed by a pitch phase. This block can be repeated up to three times a day if there is an extensive set of objectives to be worked through. Multiple teams and multiple blocks will give you dozens of refined concepts and hundreds of fledgling ideas. A common movie poster delivery is even more critical when this quantity of ideas is produced.

Focused periods of brainstorming need inspiration space around them. Your participants need time to charge up their brainstorm batteries.

More on that next.

In Brief

• Keep brainstorming simple. Simple ways to generate ideas are accessible and more productive for more people. Rules without complexity.

• Use the 5 & 25 plan. Intro, Ideate, Interrogate, interpret.

• Build teams with breadth, in a location where they can focus.

• Use a moderator to steer and support the teams.

• Build a movie poster suitable to be presented to a group. The right punchy info to sell a compelling story.

• Present ideas, record, repeat.

CHAPTER EIGHT

The Calm Between the Storms

Singular brainstorms are straightforward to manage and setup. A small group, some space and some props...off we go.

Once you've done one and got into the flow of your hour block and the 5 & 25 plan, it doesn't feel an effort.

Skills develop.

You may begin to play around and adapt the script.

You might use the process frequently with a small group.

You might not need the big pitch with only one team (although you could bring in others not involved in the brainstorm).

You may get team B to brainstorm the topic that team A just pitched to see if there are inspirational ideas they could build on.

As a reminder, ensure the super-duper new system has a purpose and isn't a tool that adds complexity and confusion. It's the ideas and not the process to create them that wins the prize.

Bigger brainstorms, particularly those with multiple blocks of one hour need a little more management. People moving around, lots of movie posters to manage, more themes to come up with alongside increasingly tired participants.

A brainstorm block with creation and pitch phases could run to two hours depending on the number of teams who pitch at the end. The realities of a day? You'll get no more than three blocks completed.

We feel good about our brainstorm block setups. The spaces before, between and after can't simply be a reset of new flipchart paper though. There's some surround sound needed to add greater depth to what we make in those focused blocks.

A day of creative inspiration

There's a holistic view to take here. A plan of the day with blocks of brainstorming, peppered with shorter moments to spark the creative thinking.

Morning ice breakers as the diverse teams are setup.

Activities to awaken all from the after-lunch food coma.

CHALLENGE: In fifteen minutes. Who can make the tallest self-supporting structure out of a marshmallows and cocktail sticks?

CHALLENGE: In fifteen minutes, brand your team. Here's a collection of fabric pens, baseball caps and miscellaneous craft 'stuff'. What's your team name? Design a logo and make some merchandise. Present yourselves to the group. For the rest of the day you are 'TEAM ULTRA POWER NINJA' and not Team B.

CHALLENGE: In fifteen minutes, build a bridge. Using <u>only</u> paper from the photocopier, make a bridge spanning across two feet between two blocks. The bridge that takes the greatest weight in the center is the winner.

A visiting speaker is also a good addition to the morning. Someone from a parallel industry. Someone that had similar challenges or success. Perhaps a consumer expert. An insights leader to help inform new thinking. Someone external to your company without the insular baggage of your corporation.

Your consumer experiences hundreds of stories, brands and products every day, only one or two of which may be yours. There's some useful context here of the wider, real world.

A full creative day could shape up like this:

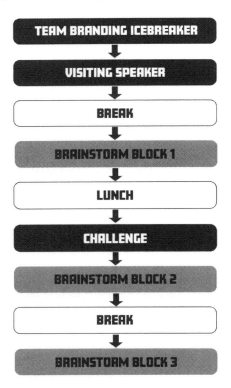

Then go to the bar.

Plussing and Plussing

The teams in the brainstorm were powerful. Together they utilized idea superpowers to originate and refine great ideas.

Without knowing it, they also used a lite version of plussing.

So, what is it? Simply put, it's taking an existing idea and building directly on it.

In a brainstorm, we hear a good idea and naturally evolve it during the conversation.

We take an idea and add features or something that makes it better, or 'plus it up', as the phrase goes.

To get the most out of plussing, we avoid saying "it's sounds good but..." (i.e. it's not really good, I'm just being polite), we say "it sounds good <u>and</u> we could add this...."

The next person says, "<u>and</u> it could do this...",

"<u>and</u> we could buy it here" for example.

We keep going until we've run out of adds which may take a while.

It's a good method to democratize an idea. Everyone contributes to the idea with their differing viewpoints and specialisms. It reinforces the iterative concept of building a good idea into a great one. Everyone is actively looking for the positive in every idea and every comment is framed with the intention of improving it further.

This should be natural, it's not a linear 'it's my turn to plus now', anyone can jump in and add and add again. Get the right 'plusses' from the right person, at the right time. If a couple of people bounce plusses between themselves for a while, then so be it.

Get the ideas written down as they emerge, sticky notes added on top of each other if you like. If the momentum drops, throw in an open positive question such as "what's a great way of selling that?" to jump start an area that might not have been 'plussed' yet.

Plussing can be used naturally as part of the brainstorm block, the one-day project or used as a snappy tool in isolation.

Once plussed, we have a richer idea we can share more widely, ready for feedback.

In Brief

• Broaden brainstorms into wider and more immersive creative days.

• Add moments to build team identity and momentum.

• Structure time to relax and regroup.

• Get external perspective. New ideas and thinking from visiting teams or individuals can spark something new for you.

• Take a great idea and plus it, plus it and plus it. There is always more that can be added to build a richer solution.

CHAPTER NINE

Sharing is Selling

Share the idea. No matter what the idea, there comes a time when it gets shared with the world. That 'world' might be a boss, the end consumer or your team.

We're at the 'milestone', 'check-in, 'review' or 'crit' (the critique).

This stage isn't some tick box. It's selling.

We may not have a truck load of goods for consumers to purchase, we may only have a 'sketch' idea, a killer PowerPoint deck, or 10 minutes in front of a passive crowd. Whatever the environment or the format, we are still asking others to buy the idea.

The 'selling' of an idea can be a tough gig. There may be others with ideas to sell, limited budgets, short time or no resources available. We need to sell and sell well.

As with the design brief, walking into a room and beginning with an outcome plan is a solid start. What is the perfect result of this selling event? Once you know that, all the language you use, the visuals to guide and the focus of any conversations is clear. You can own the process and make sure you ultimately steer the event and sell what you want, in the way you want to.

Script the story you want them to read

We are back at this again. No-one will buy when you simply stand up in front of them and ask 'how many do you want' as you hold your product in the air.

Revealing your idea like this is just like you asking your audience to read out the last page of a book or watching the last 2 minutes of a movie or play. It just doesn't make sense, there's no context.

Your idea needs a storyline, it needs context before you reveal the final page and the crowd buy.

We're at the movies once more, but not with our brainstorm movie poster this time. In this movie we're building a well-structured story of locations, actors and props. A narrative to give our idea context. A place, an audience and our idea, all in context.

The movie story selling tool gives us a massive solution. The one big problem all great new ideas face...they've simply never existed before.

There's no reason why your boss, your team or whoever your selling to, needs it. They've all managed without your idea before. This unfamiliarity and newness can be a real barrier. It's risky and a challenge.

Take your audience on a journey with you. Don't teleport them to the destination. Don't reveal that last part of the story as you walk in the room with your product held aloft in your hand. Even the bravest audience will struggle to get behind your idea if you don't take them with you on a story.

A to Z

Start with the familiar and take incremental steps further away.

Start with a reminder of the problem today that you're solving tomorrow. "Last year we didn't deliver the numbers by 20%, I have a solution to rectify that this year."

We've simply anchored everyone to today and the need. Your objective is clear and it's important enough that everyone should listen.

Reference to what is known or exists already is great. We're connecting to the familiar, demonstrating a path to the new future state. Your audience may be open-minded, but too many steps or jumps away from today can confuse and alienate.

You can't transport an audience too many steps away from today's reality in one go. Build anchor steps that are relatable as you take them on the path to innovation.

Take a step, reference back.

Take another step and another, reference back.

At every new stage we're on, or close to, familiar solid ground.

We can continue those steps to move closer and closer to our innovative idea. Closer to the idea that was originally so far away and tough for our audience to understand.

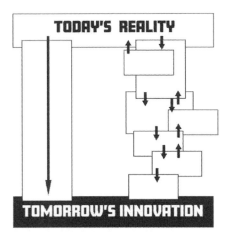

Product design deals with these types of steps all the time. Technology moves fast, there needs to be a story path to take your consumer on. If they don't 'get it' or feel unsure on its use, then it doesn't get picked up. A great idea with real benefits can easily be lost.

"It was ahead of its time." No, it wasn't sold correctly. The need and benefit weren't communicated.

Sell the problem, sell the need, sell the solution

In no way is this about restricting the amount of innovation or how far ahead of where we are now, you should target.

It's simply that the story you tell must fully explain the path to get there and the benefits. A solution that may feel far away, needs more steps to get there. Dropping a car into the 19th century without the story, context and human centered benefit around it is just confusing. If you're bringing something new to the table, something to change thinking or the way we do things, you need context and a journey.

Contextual stories endure. For example, you own a car with its power measured in 'horsepower'. If we were all honest, I think we'd struggle to quantify what a 'horsepower' is without 2 minutes on the internet.

If I was in the late 19th century and owned a horse, and someone offered me a device that had lots of horsepower(s) I'd get it. This is quantifiable to what I have now. 10 times more powerful than my four-legged friend tied to that post over there. That means I can work faster. Problem, need, solution. A simple piece of storytelling and context that makes the adoption of this new idea of 'the car' easier to sell.

Quantifying improvement in your story based on current standards is an easy and accessible way of communicating a benefit when you sell an idea.

We're in 2001. Music is on cassettes, vinyl and compact discs. I've got boxes full of them.

Suddenly, an idea emerges that a music player in my pocket can hold thousands of albums. This is as tangible and relatable as that car and that horse. The sales pitch then wasn't about the best tech specs. No mention of the average megabytes for each song, bitrates and technological leaps in my pocket. What was presented and sold was

71

'album capacity', the bridge back to the familiar. All I needed to clearly know was that I could have every song I own, when I want it. Problem, need, solution.

Today, that hard drive has moved to the other side of the world and has every song ever recorded on it. Ownership and storage now become renting and streaming. Innovation built on invention.

The simple story of digital music is clear, the sales pitch has taken me from the relatable and familiar into a fundamentally new future with a straightforward narrative bridge from one place to another. Ultimately, I'm still listening to the same music.

A tangible, singular link from current to future can be very understandable and easy to communicate. More complex ideas need greater clarity in our story for an audience to buy.

Sets, Characters and Props

Our story, like a movie, has characters (audience) on sets (environments) surrounded by props (products).

In a movie, those 3 simple elements are held together by a script and music score that bring them to life. They build atmosphere and lead us on a narrative journey to explain something completely new in a short time. Just like the problem we have. We have a new idea to sell in a short time.

We take this approach and build out a narrative. By the end of the movie I know why this idea you've just presented to me is something I want to buy.

Your audience have all seen movies. Your approach is familiar to them. You've spoken about people, in a place surrounded by objects and this is what we see every day.

No leap of imagination from your audience is needed. No figuring out your presentation before they understand what you're presenting.

The good news with this type of storytelling is you don't need to be some Hollywood director or murder-mystery author to write it. The likelihood is you've already auditioned your cast, scouted your locations, and shopped a few props as part of your idea creation process.

Using the same story beats you used to create your ideas in the first place, gives you a jumpstart on the selling story and you get continuity in both product and message. If the reason you designed a product was for a certain purpose, place or audience, simply use that same reasoning to sell it.

Take the one-day brief example, you might have undertaken as part of your next new product launch – "You're on a bus, what's missing?" was the question.

Immediately we have our location. We're on the bus. We know what that feels like.

We have our cast from the driver to the passengers.

We're surrounded by the props. Windows full of everchanging scenery, graphics telling us to buy this or that, vast amounts of luggage and a few empty seats.

Perhaps we also have the high-pitched headphone soundtrack from some fellow travelers.

Your idea is the script, the missing element as per the brief.

The good news is whatever that idea, you can tell it and transport your audience to that place in a heartbeat. We know buses, the format, the environment, immediately your audience are on board with us. When you describe waiting at the stop, getting on the bus and buying your ticket they know what that feels like. You don't need to spend valuable time explaining the stage/people and props in depth. That moment when your idea fulfilled a need on that journey, I get that. I was there.

We can continue to layer up the storytelling.

What are the interactions with our cast on the bus? That kid wearing that cool looking T shirt that reminds me of that radio station that just rebranded. The Dad reading the crime novel by that author that wrote the free short story you read online.

Building out a set, with cast and props gives us a place to play. We have a jump start in familiarity to sell our idea story.

Keep those stories simple and familiar to all your audience. Talking to kids? An older generation? A sub-section of an industry? Plant them in a place they all know. Sell the problem they can all see in that place. Sell the need they all have there. Sell your solution.

Regardless of the complexity and level of your innovation, this is a straightforward way to make idea leaps more easily understood.

Buyers become great sellers

I firmly believe your best customers are your existing customers. This is the cornerstone of brand advocacy. I liked your product (and service) X, I'm going to be interested in your future product Y or Z. These are the first people we should be engaging with. They are far more than 'warm' contact or an easy sell.

Those buyers become part of your salesforce with every purchase. They endorse and recommend to others. A review online or word of mouth. Now more than ever, that social proof and endorsement or review can easily steer another purchase from a stranger. The opportunity to see and hear from others who have purchased has never been easier or more global.

This is great if you're selling a final product. It also works much earlier than that and even in smaller teams, at an idea stage.

Early on in our idea journey we share and sell. Right at the end of our first brainstorm day we shared and sold to the wider group. We got votes to show our idea was great. That was a purchase. They bought into your idea. Those who voted for you are advocates for you and the idea. Big team or small, we're building a group of idea buyers who will become idea sellers as we develop and progress the concept. There's momentum here.

We sell multiple times in this process. We may be selling to get budget approved. Selling an idea to a senior team.

Much like that expansive email list of consumers your company may have, keep track of your 'idea buyers'. Those that like your idea(s). Talk to them, engage with them to sell your ideas further.

In Brief

• Sharing is selling. Sharing turns buyers into sellers for you.

• Sell with familiarity. With tangible, relatable benefits that solve a problem and deliver against a need.

• Plant your idea in a story. Re-use the story and the locations from your idea generation as places to transplant your buyers too. They can see the problem first-hand and how your idea is a strong solution.

• More than ever, the actions of others buying is visible for the world to see. Those advocates are critical as social proof for your idea.

• Sell the problem, sell the need, sell the solution.

CHAPTER TEN

The Edit

We're in the wild now. We've created an idea and placed a compelling contextual story around it.

There's amazing thinking and a wondrous narrative that your audience clearly understand. Now, you hold your idea product aloft.

Feedback, comments, questions and scrutiny.

In my 20 years designing and creating for brands, every single project and idea has gone through this stage, so you should expect it too. More than expect it, you should encourage it.

I was part of project to integrate new brands into my design team as part of a restructure. A big all-day meeting, lots of people. The team 'handing over' did a great job. They presented what they did clearly, how and why they did it and plans for future ideas for the brands. They took us on the brand journey and built out the stories around them brilliantly, we got it.

We reviewed what they had done, and they knew their stuff, they set up the narrative and the needs nicely. Feedback? "All very positive" we said, feeling good. Bar?

What didn't work?

The head of the group handing over said "What didn't work?" in front of everyone from his team who had just presented. Err.

"Great to hear you liked the plan, but what didn't work for you? The team are all here, we can fix it." Then came glancing around and quite a long pause.

It was the first time I'd come across such a direct ask for what you might traditionally call 'negative' feedback, particularly given the thorough presentation that left us with such a positive reaction.

The reality was we had an overall good feeling about what we'd seen, but being asked the very specific detail question, of what could have been better made us think again.

We were never going to have a laundry list of things to change but sure enough, one question sparked a couple of comments on refining ideas for the future. Given this was an area we would need to advocate and 'buy into', there were solid points made.

Without the quest for deeper feedback, for 'negative' feedback, we would never have had the discussion around those issues and fixed them, with everyone who mattered in the room. There was no animosity, no risk to anyone personally.

Positive feedback is great, we feel good and it's 'easy', no need to confront or to challenge. The reality is whilst the positive is good, it serves only to reinforce what we know; that our idea is a good one. At its core it works. We may take a confidence boost from that, but 'negative' feedback is actionable. We have something that we can do that can make the idea even better, more resilient to greater scrutiny later.

Questioning and comment is critical, it stress tests the thought process. Our buyers need it to be better, more confident and successful sellers later.

You've lived with your idea since its inception. Others have only just learned of it. There's a learning curve here you should expect and help along.

Pitch with vigor, receive with thanks

Idea creation can be an immensely personal thing and receiving comments on them can feel personal too.

You've invested your time and effort to bring something new to life.

You believe in it.

You've stood up in front of your audience and presented the reason for this idea to exist, the need for it, you feel confident about it.

You didn't stand up and present an idea with the killer opening line "I've got an idea, it's not too bad, probably." No, you pitched and presented with vigor, to sell the idea, not to leave it on the shelf.

One tool to take the feedback constructively is to remember back to our one-day projects.

We structured our teams to avoid one common point of view. We tried to eliminate the same blind spots of thinking.

We brought teams together from a breadth of job functions and diversity of roles to ensure we had a range of ideas.

The same is true here, the feedback we're taking is simply like adding a new contributor to our team to ensure we've all got a winner. We're not being too precious.

A few days or weeks ago we wouldn't have called their comments 'feedback' or taken them with a pinch of personal attack. Those same comments would have been idea contributions. Time has passed and the context has changed, nothing more. The senior leader in our one-day project a few weeks back, who was such a good idea creator then, now becomes perceived as a 'different person', behind a desk and being presented to.

A good 'idea' given a few weeks ago from that person or team, can be translated as good 'feedback' now and taken with the same approach.

Ultimately, the idea gets improved, but some time has passed, the deadline to deliver is weeks closer.

This is where we evaluate and balance the desire to deliver.

What do those comments bring?

How essential is the edit?

Is a short term hit now to timing better than living longer term with a product that could have been better?

This is where we think again about create, update, update, update.

Do these edits sound like we're looking only for the definitive treasure? How easy is that update, update, update?

It may be new feedback gets incorporated into an update down the line, much like our app update. Just don't reject great feedback because it doesn't suit the plan.

Having said negative feedback can be an absolute gift that should be encouraged, there are times when feedback is tough to figure out. For the sake of the idea, we need to help clarify it.

Some feedback doesn't make sense.

This isn't something I can 'fix'.

Where's the action in that?

What do you mean?

How do I translate that?

But it can be quite funny when you receive the impossible feedback.

"Playful but rough, but also epic but quite modest at the same time."

Keep up with hovering art directors, Adobe Inc. YouTube 2017

The ads from the creative software company Adobe sum up the perils of feedback and idea guidance brilliantly. Our feedback givers may want to evoke feelings and aspirations in our ideas, but they aren't directions we action, they are outcomes. An ability to take a step back from those aspirations and understand what can create them is needed.

When you pose the question; "Any feedback?" you'll get answers.

When you get those answers, ask more questions to truly drill down into the details. To capture the aspirations, yes. But to also truly inform the practicalities to get there. There's a skill to that questioning and to delivering great feedback in the first place. More on that next.

In Brief

• Encourage all feedback from your audience.

• Feedback now can be treated in the same way as an idea contribution, earlier in the process.

• Evaluate feedback that may disrupt timings. Can you incorporate it in an update later? How critical is its inclusion in the idea at launch?

• Ideas can be full of personal effort and energy. While comments may feel personal, always consider the strength of the idea and remove the personal where you can.

• Ask your audience specifically for negative feedback. They may feel broadly happy with the idea, but there are always details to be improved.

CHAPTER ELEVEN

Actionable Feedback

Can that black logo be a little less dark?

You mean make it grey? No, still black, just a little less dark.

We've invested a good deal of time honing our idea generation skills. We are adept at creating and selling ideas and have an amazing ability to bring ideas to life. Our colleagues though, need our help.

Members of our team may not have had that idea experience. We script our narrative and present it and listen with anticipation for the feedback to build our idea even stronger.

"I don't like it."

"I don't like green, nor does my wife."

Or the best one...silence.

It's here we help, both us and them. There is a craft and skill to giving great feedback in the same way we can learn how to take it.

Great feedback helps the idea. It's in everyone's interest to have a better idea. Where we can, we should help others give feedback and to refine it into actionable steps.

Sometimes there's another issue, feedback is too specific, it's all about the action, not the outcome.

"Can you make that purple?"

Of course, we can...but why? What's the need we're solving for? The approach is the same, let's get underneath the words of the comment and discover the issue. Then we can craft the right solution.

Every job type has its own vocabulary. Some technical and specific. Some emotional and broad. Great feedback involves flexing your style into that of the person you're giving feedback to.

Flexing styles

To take this to an extreme, this is a language learning exercise. If you were talking to someone who spoke a different language, no amount of feedback in your language would help.

You can't learn a new feedback language (or teach it) in the middle of your presentation either.

The time for this language learning is before you need to have a critical conversation using it.

Get teams together before, and detail what makes great feedback to you.

How to phrase.

How to help you understand what they are feeling.

Broad brush direction, or specific details?

Talking the same 'language of feedback' can really cut through the ambiguity and negativity that is so often associated with it. You've demonstrated you see so much value in their comments, that you want to really understand them fully.

There are times where that type of language learning might be tough. New clients, new teams, a bigger group.

In this case, we all start from a position that feedback is there to make an idea stronger. We're looking for more info that can often be difficult to articulate. We need to guide and extract richer answers as we question our feedback giver.

Avoid the 'closed' questions. Anything you can answer in a single word or two is closed.

"I don't like green". Feedback.

"Instead of that color, would you like blue instead?" No. "Red", No. Closed.

We may be here sometime as we run through a rainbow of options. We're throwing darts trying to hit a target and we might need a lot to hit the right spot.

In place of those closed questions we use open questions that get broader feedback to interpret and delve more deeply into. Then we drop in the focused 'closed' question at the end for confirmation.

"What are the challenges you see with this color?" Cue a set of comments, with far more flavor and description, something more that you can dive further into and ultimately fix.

Keep going on the open questions until you feel confident you've got the detail. Then finish with the closed question to wrap it up. "So, purple would be perfect then?" Yes.

Other times, silence rings out across the room.

"I'd welcome your point of view in the color choice in particular." Steer the conversation into areas that you know may be a problem or may have been something you've been concerned about. See if others share the concern.

As the conversation flows, look for common ground, consistency. One set of feedback may not be shared more widely by others in the room. Some may be reluctant to contradict in an open forum, or against someone more senior. In this case, you can help by simply transferring the feedback to you and then putting it back into the room.

"If I were to present that idea now painted red, how would others in the room feel about it?"

It's me presenting the color option. I'm inviting the wider team to contribute. I'm not starting a conflict amongst my audience. I'll take the heat for the good of the idea.

There are times where your audience are truly split. No unified feedback. Team X want this idea and team Y another one. Even in the same team there may be division.

"This logo must be yellow."

"This logo must be red."

We could make it orange then nobody wins.

At the point of absolute contrasting views, comes the moment where the art of truly stress-testing the feedback comes in.

The goal here is to strip away the personal elements to any feedback. Analyze the reasons behind it. Evaluate the strength, importance and impact of it.

"If this was red, we'd launch late."

OK we can evaluate that impact.

"If it was yellow, we'd sell 10% more."

Why is that?

Quantify the reasons and the impacts. Have the debate amongst the groups.

What is more important to keep?

What is important to your consumer?

Will what you're asking to be changed make any difference to them at all? If not, why are you changing it?

Time and edits go hand in hand. An edit that isn't always focused on the consumer is simply wasted time and money. We are editing for ourselves. Regardless of team structures and priorities, selling more of the product from your company benefits everyone. There's a collective responsibility to keep focused on that objective.

Your team 'winning' the argument to make it red, with negative impacts for your consumer and fewer sales for all, is a loss for everyone.

In Brief

• Every job function has its own language. Take time to learn others and to teach your audience what great feedback sounds like to you. Just do this before the presentation.

• Use open questions to delve more deeply into feedback and get to the root of the issue. Use a closed question to anchor the decision at the end.

• Prompt questions on a specific subject if you're met with silence by your audience when you ask for feedback.

• In times of a split audience, there is a need for evaluation of consequences of each direction. Remove the personal preference and observe the effect of the decisions on your end consumer only.

CHAPTER TWELVE

The Sticky Idea

Faded Newness. Last year's phone is so...last year.

That must-watch TV show from 12 months ago is feeling tired on series 9.

The great idea that worked so well, just won't work now. The world has moved on. That was quick.

We're surrounded by the noise of the new in technology, products and ideas.

It's easy to be caught up in this relentless wave of newness, the craving to have the latest idea. New products a research group loved.

Our 'What's new' culture has implications for anyone who originates ideas. That great concept from your one-day project last year might need a refresh, consumers are moving on.

When we appraise the process for our own idea refreshes, we need to be mindful of being 'Sticky'.

Sticky in 2 ways:

1) "We've seen company X launch a new thing using this method, we should do the same, let's get some ideas to match."

We're sticking closely to someone else's (current) plan. We're sticking to their timing, method and product.

2) "Our product from last year sold so well. I think it will sell well next year too."

We're sticking to what we have without considering if there's still a need, and therefore if it's still a winner.

Both sticky situations can be equally risky. With our competitor's ideas we're not doing what they do. We're doing it later and to our brand story, not theirs. We've lost the time it takes to design, develop, market and sell too. We're using last year's approach to a world that has already experienced that earlier product. Why do they need it from you again?

Keeping a legacy product too long and feeling complacent in our success is the other path. In a world of rapid changes, the environment for our success may have altered.

This may sound like common sense, nothing lasts forever. Fading brand names and legacy ideas that were huge though, are proof of this issue. Fond memories of renting VHS tapes and posting them through a returns window of a closed store spring to mind.

A need before a sale

The key to unsticking yourself from this situation is clear. At every opportunity, look at your consumer need first and not at what you have available to sell them.

Just because you have thousands of stores, stuffed full of magnetic tapes and pricey popcorn doesn't mean that's what your consumers want, now.

You're not in the plastic tapes business, you're in the home entertainment business. "I'm at home and I want to watch a movie now, how do I do it?" it sounds like a one-day project to me, that should have been done in 2005.

Perhaps it should now be "I'm at home and I want to watch a movie now, while the rest of the family watch their own movies in other rooms !". The jump from shelf to stream is old news.

New devices.

New apps.

New ways of watching.

New ways of paying.

New corporations with sky-high valuations.

New ways for old corporations to resell their content library.

Once you know what your customers need, you can create a solution for them.

It wasn't overnight that video tapes started to leave those stores in fewer numbers. Those numerous streaming platforms didn't come online all at once. New types of screens appeared in households gradually. Mobile phone use had a clear upward trend for years before eventually overtaking home phone use.

There's time to adapt and innovate and to see a trend in consumers and their needs, don't feel it's too late to start.

There's no need to jump from one area of business to another either. Look at the trends, the world your consumer inhabits, and adapt as needed. Just do that review now.

If you're starting with what you must sell, you'll spend all your time looking for a consumer to sell it to.

It's a hard sale too. You'll spend a disproportionate amount of time selling to those who don't really want the idea, while you try and find those who do.

Instead, spend the bulk of the time understanding and finding your consumer and developing the idea for them. Easier selling follows, you're giving them what they need and want.

A blank sheet of paper

Ask yourself a simple question, often.

"If I had a blank sheet of paper, would I develop the product/idea/service I have now, for next year's consumer?"

If the answer is no and you weren't planning to revisit what you have now, you're sticky. You're sticking to what you have available to sell and not to fulfil need.

Asking such a direct question, no caveats, removes all the structure associated to your current idea. For now, we're evaluating the strength of the idea in isolation and not the ecosystem around it. The current workforce in those video stores, the video stores themselves, or the processes or challenges of any change. We've removed any emotional attachment and legacy we may have had to the current idea.

This is a focus on whether the idea is right for the consumer.

Even more deeply than that, would you jump through the hoops of development to create it now? All that time and cost to develop it. Is the idea you have worth that? If it's not, is it worth holding onto now?

Rarely in business do you get the chance to start with such a blank sheet of paper. You can't simply turn an idea or part of a business off. You can't invent the next piece of movie streaming technology overnight.

This creative process to evaluate an idea can be done easily though. It should be done frequently too.

The clarity of this abstract is that it becomes a starting point to figure out what should be on that blank piece of paper. At least you know you have an issue.

You can begin to understand what your consumers do want next year.

You start to understand their true needs.

The path to that consumer need then becomes the challenge for the year. We start to add back in the realities, the people and the stores you removed to get that clarity in the first place.

The great thing is you have an objective, much like the script and story we setup earlier

Back to our blank paper. The answer was yes. I would develop the idea we have now. Great, knowing you're aligned to your consumers, and that the idea resonates and delivers against their needs allows space to innovate further.

You've taken the time to check what your customers want without the cost and change of idea redevelopment, so you can have the confidence to double down on the idea you have. Perhaps there's an iteration, an update, update, update process, to get it closer to the end of the rainbow.

Sticky ideas aren't just limited to the big themes and products of your business. They can be scaled to evaluate a process, a team structure or a way of working and beyond.

"If I had a blank sheet of paper, would I use this process I have now, for next year?"

"If I had a blank sheet of paper, would I structure the team the way I have now, for next year?"

If you can clearly identify the need, whether consumer or internally business related, then this technique gets rid of the stickiness.

In Brief

• As time passes, evaluate if your idea would be right for your consumer next year. Current success is no guarantee of future success.

• Ask yourself often "If I had a blank sheet of paper, would I develop the product/service I have now, for next year's consumer?".

• Build a business plan that factors in frequent updates. You should know you'll need a version two before you launch version one.

• Remove the ecosystem around your current idea. Evaluating just the strength of the idea and not the legacy infrastructure will remove the tendency to be sticky.

• Always focus on the needs of your consumer, the trends in the world around them and the impact of future technology.

• Avoid following and sticking to your competitors' path. What you see is dated and aligned to their brand and story strategy, not yours.

CONCLUSION

Ideas are truly magical things. Magical things that we can all spark into life with some *Rocket Thinking*.

Throughout this book, my goal was to bring to life the processes and tools that make such thinking real.

Real processes that are practical and usable now. The same processes I've used in more than 20 years in the idea business. Idea tools that win. Tools that you can win with too.

You've discovered that originating ideas, building out stories around them and constructing a framework to support them are skills that can be learned, honed and shared.

We start our script, make our movie, cast our actors and build our props. We listen to our consumers, but also interrogate them to filter the perceived reality they may present.

We pique our curiosity. Our heads up from screens to truly observe, interpret and morph the great ideas that exist all around us already.

We invite others on our bus to experience and edit the story of the idea we're building. When we drive up to an obstacle, we know how to find that route around.

In just one day we can jolt our thinking. We ignite a new idea or feed an existing one. One day to experience all that a larger project might throw at us. One day to visualize that winning kick so early in the match.

We're here to help our colleagues too. We have the tools to gather our teams together to build a fluid place in which to create new ideas. After a tower of marshmallows and a simple one-hour block of creating ideas, we can generate a theatrical masterpiece, complete with movie poster.

We add to and 'plus-up' the ideas of others. We layer diverse viewpoints, experience and knowledge to make a rich and positive idea, quickly.

We encourage the critical, we want it to make a better idea. We learn a common language of feedback and frame it into something that we can use. We help others help us.

These are tangible tools we can all use right now.

They are not the sole property of 'the creative' that you may know.

They are not something so delicate that we can't mash them up or edit them to suit our needs better.

Not so precious that we feel we can't use them often.

Not so complex that the process gets in the way of outcome.

Your consumers buy the end idea, they don't buy the process you used to create them. You know what it takes to get there, they don't.

We know our idea has been sold multiple times during its life. Before that transactional finale. The scrutiny of our many buyers evolving into endorsements as the idea develops. Buyers are sellers for us.

We've enriched our story at every stage of purchase. We've made a more complete narrative as we take it to market. We've leveraged the familiar and the parallel as we present. We bridge with steps to the innovative, regardless of the distance to be spanned. Our buyers understand the path, the benefit.

We understand our consumer. We understand their problems, their needs. We deliver a solution.

We evaluate the data, understanding beyond the numerical. We look for the innovation, the shift. Not just the simple adaption of our daily car journey.

We see our competition launching as we edit, evolve and release our version two and three. We inch towards the treasure with every version. We create, update, update, update.

We know the idea we have now, so successful today, may become sticky soon. All we need is a piece of paper to understand that.

My objective with the book was idea superpowers for you, now.

I hope these pages have delivered easy-to-use powers that constantly drive new idea creation and success for you.

Remember the questions I asked in the introduction? How does the movie director, that tech company, that franchise owner making fan T-shirts, deliver repeated success?

I've been in the room as each of those ideas were being developed.

We used the same idea superpowers that are in this book. Identical.

These tools work regardless of your industry or objective. Tools that are applicable across organizations, teams and locations. Time and budget aren't limiting factors to activating them.

Try them.

Share them.

Be inspired by them. Ignite your own *Rocket Thinking.* Now.

-End-

In the spirit of always wanting to iterate and build on good ideas and to share information across a community of Rocket Thinkers, it would mean a great deal to me if you could spare the time to leave a review for the book on Amazon.

Thank you.

-

FREE SUPPORTING MATERIAL

As a small token of thanks for buying this book, I've created a free and sparky PDF full of practical info to help ignite your own *Rocket Thinking*.

Complementing the tools in this book, these easy to grab and use pages distil key processes and techniques into at-a-glance worksheets and templates.

I've seen first-hand how valuable these can be in amplifying the thinking, managing the process and delivering outstanding results.

Sign up for free to The Rocket List and download your own *Rocket Thinking* materials here:

AndrewWoolnough.com/PBfree

ABOUT THE AUTHOR

Andrew Woolnough has been originating, developing and bringing great ideas to life for more than 20 years.

From family movies and TV shows, toys and consumer products, and from utility suppliers to pharmaceutical companies, it's very likely Andrew's ideas and the successful products from them have made it into your home.

He has led in-house global design teams for multi-nationals and lived both in the UK and US. He continues to work with ambitious brands and companies, amplifying their idea generation techniques through workshops and driving their creative delivery, product development and marketing functions.

Andrew is a graduate of both the University of Plymouth in the UK and of London's prestigious Royal College of Art where he graduated as a Master of Arts, Industrial Design.

He is a sought-after creative consultant and frequent speaker at creative industry events. He regularly shares the power of ideas, brand storytelling and proven strategies for creative thinking with teams around the world.

AndrewWoolnough.com

NOTES

Printed in Great Britain
by Amazon